MW01243497

This Notebook Belongs To

Made in the USA
Middletown, DE
30 April 2022

65041640R00068